CEO & Creative Direction: Steve Rad
Project Manager: Jordyn Van De Keere
Art Direction: Ingrid Chow
Design & Illustration: Ingrid Chow, Mel Chan, Fraser Aberdeen, Dionysis Zogaris, Hanna Stefan
Photo & Video: Rami Mikhail, Antonio Padron
Bill Nye Photography: Jesse DeFlorio, Brandon Hill, Bill Miles
Composite Artist: Adrian Sommeling
Editorial: Eleanor Rose, Bill Nye
Sourcing & Production: Jack Xing, Philip Tien
App Design & Interface: Jeff Dotson, Tony Fouts, Brian Massey, Christopher Brown, Jacob Jetter, Jeremy Schaefer, Ryan Hanson, Austin Hancock
Content & Licensing: Levin Nelson
Animation: Daniel Mandina, Eirenarch Sese
Talent: Nik Sommeling, Meijs Binnendijk, Viola Abley, Alexander Rad

UPC: 850009794802
ISBN: 978-1-951090-21-0

Manufactured in China

Patent # 10430658, 10558858, 10565452

Edition: 01.NYE94802.0623

This edition published in 2023 by
Abacus Brands, Inc.
5501 Balcones Dr., Suite A211,
Austin, TX 78731

This edition printed for Books Are Fun 2023.

Special thanks to: Jackie McCoy-Rad, Alexander Maxwell Rad, Ayla Jordan Rad, Nick Pampenella, Ennis Kamcili, Shelly Marchetti, David Evenchick.

INTERACTIVE EXPERIMENT BOOK

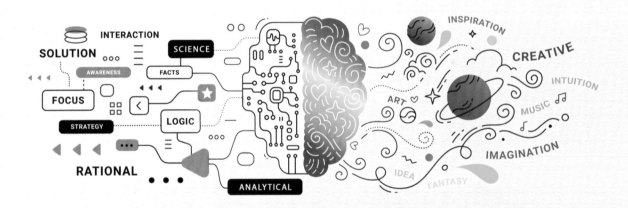

PRODUCTS DESIGNED TO ACTIVATE BOTH THE ANALYTICAL AND CREATIVE SIDES OF THE BRAIN

@ABACUSBRANDS
ABACUSBRANDS.COM

CONTENTS

GETTING STARTED

1

Download the **BILL NYE'S VR SCIENCE KIT** app. When ready, hit **START** and select a **PLAY MODE**.

PLEASE READ CAREFULLY!

2

HANDHELD

AUGMENTED REALITY
(yellow options)

Best for AR pop ups and step-by-step lessons and tutorials. This mode is also ideal for those with motion sickness.

GOGGLES

VIRTUAL REALITY
(red options)

Use the viewer when triggering red hotspots in the book, taking you to an immersive world in 360° virtual reality.

AUTO

MIXED REALITY (AR+VR)
(yellow and red options)

We'll tell you when to hold your device for AR and when to put on the viewer for VR.

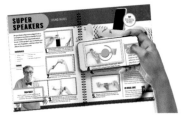

Use the blue dot (reticle) as a cursor to point and load either AR (yellow) or VR (red) options.

Don't sit too close. The app needs to see both the left and right pages at the same time.

Note: Lay the book as flat as possible.

Do not put on the viewer until instructed!

USING YOUR VR VIEWER

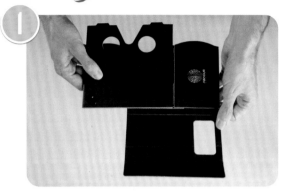

Unfold the front flap and lay open. Pop the body up into a square shape.

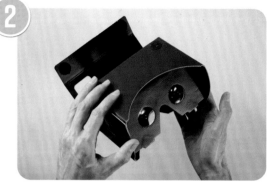

Fold the lens flap down into the square body, and pop the tabs into the slots.

When instructed to put on the viewer, place your device into the front pocket with the screen facing the lenses. Make sure your camera is positioned towards the flap opening.

Fold the front flap over the body and secure the velcro. Use the suction cups to secure your device in place.

NOTE

- Give the app permission to use your camera.
- Be sure your ringer switch is on and not set to silent.
- Turn up your brightness.
- Disable auto-brightness to prevent dimming during the experience.
- Wipe smudges and fingerprints from your device.
- Use standard or mid-size phones as larger devices may not fit properly.
- Remove your phone's protective case when possible.

TIPS & TRICKS

GENERAL SAFETY

- Read and follow these instructions, the safety rules, and the first aid information, and keep for reference.

- Avoid watching more than 10 minutes of VR content consecutively as extended use can lead to eye strain. Looking at digital devices too long can make your eyes sore, itchy, tired, or watery.

- Wash hands before and after carrying out projects. Clean all equipment after use.

- The incorrect use of materials can cause injury.

- Liquid coloring will stain clothing and surfaces. Handle with caution and with adult supervision. When possible, lay down paper towels, newspaper, napkins or do projects outdoors.

- Some projects are messy but fun! We suggest wearing old, scrappy clothes when handling liquid coloring.

FIRST AID

- In the event of a burn, run the affected area under cold water for five minutes. Do not apply ice directly to the skin as this can cause further damage. Seek medical attention, if necessary.

- In the event of a cut, hold pressure on the injured area to reduce bleeding. Wash with water and apply a bandage. Seek medical attention, if necessary.

- In the event of a fall or other injury, seek medical attention.

- If a substance gets in an eye or cut, flush with water immediately. Seek medical attention, if necessary.

FREQUENTLY ASKED QUESTIONS

 Which devices are compatible?
Mobile devices with iOS 9 / Android 13 or greater are compatible. Tablets can be used for AR full screen lessons, but we do not recommend using them for VR experiences as they do not fit inside the viewer.

 Why did Bill Nye stop or disappear?
The app is actively scanning the book to recognize and load content specific to the page you're on, so if you look away, it will think you are done with the experience. Keep your device pointed at the book, or flip to a new page to change the experience.

 Why do some experiences crash, not load, or give me a black screen?
Our apps require some power to run, so please shut down other apps running in the background as they often fight for energy with our programs.

 Why is the image blurry in the viewer?
Be sure to only use the viewer when instructed, upon activating red VR targets in the book. A common mistake is putting the viewer on too early when the image is still in full screen AR mode.

 How do I exit virtual reality?
When in VR, a floating "exit" button can be found near your feet in the viewer. Use the blue dot in the center of the screen to point and activate the exit feature.

HAVING TROUBLE? WATCH THE VIDEO TUTORIAL TO GET STARTED.

Visit us online at abacusbrands.com for more frequently asked questions, or email us directly at **support@abacusbrands.com** to troubleshoot any issues you may be experiencing. We are happy to help!

MATERIALS

Below you'll find a list of materials. Gather them now or at the start of each project.

- [ ] Ball-tipped pin or sewing needle
- [ ] Magnet
- [ ] Small piece of Styrofoam
- [ ] Bowl
- [ ] Water
- [ ] Two chairs or objects of the same height
- [ ] 3 pieces of string, each about 10 inches (25 cm) long
- [ ] 2 washers
- [ ] Straw
- [ ] Tape
- [ ] 3 balloons
- [ ] Wax crayon
- [ ] Hard-boiled egg in shell
- [ ] Beaker or measuring cup
- [ ] Vinegar
- [ ] Spoon
- [ ] Old toothbrush
- [ ] Washable school glue
- [ ] Red and blue liquid coloring
- [ ] Baking soda
- [ ] Saline solution (contact lens solution containing boric acid and sodium borate)
- [ ] Shallow dish
- [ ] Black pepper
- [ ] Liquid dish soap

- [ ] Clear bottle
- [ ] Funnel
- [ ] 2 glass cups
- [ ] Cardboard tube
- [ ] Felt pen
- [ ] Scissors
- [ ] Two paper cups
- [ ] Duct tape
- [ ] Paper towel
- [ ] 3 resealable plastic bags
- [ ] White vinegar
- [ ] Paper
- [ ] Vegetable oil
- [ ] Effervescent antacid tablet
- [ ] Ice cubes
- [ ] Plate
- [ ] Salt
- [ ] Pennies
- [ ] Tweezers
- [ ] Bottle of soda
- [ ] Rubber band
- [ ] Small mirror
- [ ] Pencil sharpener
- [ ] 4-6 Pencils
- [ ] Smartphone (required to activate AR/VR content)

NOTE
Some basic household items are required to complete projects in the book. These are listed at the start of each activity.

INTRODUCTION

Hi, I'm Bill Nye... welcome to my VR science experience!

Science is all around us, from the colors on your favorite T-shirt, to the music you listen to, everything in the world can be explained by science—well... almost everything, we're still working on some things!

In this book, I'll explain some key scientific principles through fun experiments you can try at home. We're going to explore chemical reactions, sound waves, oxidation and even dive into volcanoes and slime with the help of augmented and virtual reality. All you need is a mobile device, a few basic household items and a curious mind ready to make some discoveries!

Bill Nye is an engineer, science educator, author, actor and inventor. His passion is to help people understand the importance of science and how it makes our world work. Making science entertaining and accessible is something Bill has been doing his whole life! Most notably through his multiple Emmy award-winning show, *Bill Nye The Science Guy*, and more recently *Bill Nye Saves the World*.

As CEO of the Planetary Society, a not-for-profit and world's largest space-interest group, Bill works with the organization to empower the world's citizens to advance space science and exploration.

Bill is also the author of 12 books, including a few _New York Times_ Bestsellers. The aim of these books is to encourage evidence-based education and policy on climate change, evolution and critical thinking.

Alongside his other projects, Bill continues to fight to raise awareness of climate change and the value of critical thinking, science and reason. Through his work, Bill hopes to inspire people everywhere to change the world.

Turn the page and point your mobile device at any experiment to activate the experience as we explore the wonders of science!

QUICK COMPASS

Have you ever wondered how a compass finds north? It is because of Earth's magnetic field. In this project, we will learn about magnetism and make our own north-facing compass.

MATERIALS

- ball-tipped pin
- magnet
- small piece of Styrofoam
- bowl
- water

TIMING

10 minutes

TIP
For the best results, do this project outdoors or away from metal.

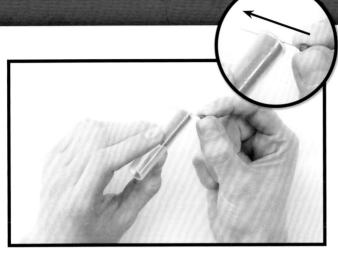

1. Carefully hold the ball of the pin. Use the magnet to rub the point of the pin in one direction, going from the middle to the end for 30-60 seconds.

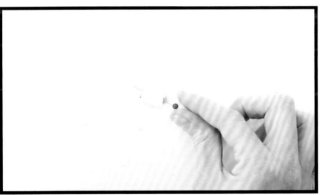

2. Break off a small piece of Styrofoam and push the magnetized pin through the center, so that equal parts of the pin are visible on both sides.

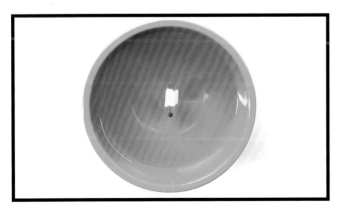

3. Fill a bowl with water. Place the Styrofoam and pin in the center of the bowl. What happens?

HOW IT WORKS

Earth has a giant **MAGNETIC FIELD** all around it. This magnetic field is strongest at the North Pole and the South Pole. The needle in a compass is a magnet that points toward the North Pole, indicating the direction of north. When you rubbed your magnet across one end of the pin, that end became **MAGNETIZED**. This made the pin spin until the magnetized end pointed north and the other end pointed south.

NOTE
Try to touch the pin to another pin or paper clip. You will see that you have created a weak magnet.

DID YOU KNOW?

You can tell directions just by looking at the position of the Sun! It generally rises in the east in the morning, and generally sets in the west in the evening.

MEMORY TRICK

Remember the four compass directions of North, East, South and West by saying Never Eat Slimy Worms. Yuck!

BALLOON ROCKET

THRUST

In order to lift off the ground and get into space, a huge rocket needs something called thrust. In this activity, we build a rocket with a balloon and use thrust to blast off!

FUN FACT

The rocket that propelled NASA's Juno spacecraft achieved a speed of over 150,000 miles per hour (240,000 km/h)!

MATERIALS

- two chairs or objects of the same height
- string
- straw
- tape
- balloon

TIMING

15 minutes

1. Position the two chairs about 10 feet (3 m) apart. Tie one end of the string to one chair and secure it tightly.

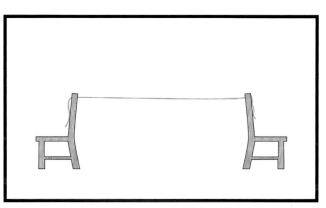

2. Measure the string to reach the second chair, leaving a little extra to tie around this chair later.
■ Cut the string.

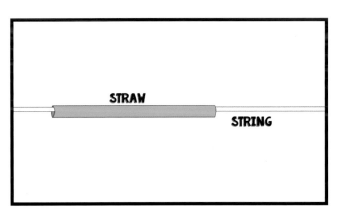

3. Thread the loose end of the string through the straw. Tie this loose end to the second chair, pulling it tight.
■ Place two pieces of tape near the middle of the straw.

4. Blow up the balloon, twist the end and then hold so the air can't escape. Use the two pieces of tape to
■ attach the balloon to the straw.

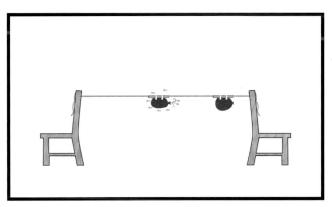

5. Without releasing the balloon, move the straw and balloon to one end of the string. Then let go of the
■ balloon. What happens?

HOW IT WORKS

The force that moves the balloon forward is called THRUST. When you let go of the end of the balloon, the air rushing backward pushes it forward along the string. This is also how rockets work. The action of the rocket's exhaust gases going fast in one direction causes the reaction of the rocket to go in the opposite direction. Rockets work in space or near the ground because of action and reaction creating thrust.

Let's talk about...
MOTION

Motion is the change in an object's position and many forces affect motion. Let's take a look at some of the factors that explain how an object moves, or doesn't move.

FORCE

Force can be a push or a pull on an object. You can't see forces but you can see their outcome—changing an object's speed, direction or shape.

INERTIA (in-ER-shuh)

You know that heavy things are harder to move around than lighter things. This property of things is called "inertia." The more inertia something has, the more force you have to use to get it moving, or get it to stop moving.

FUN FACT
A cheetah can reach speeds up to 60 mph (100 km/h).

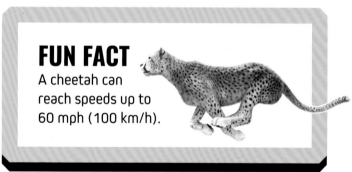

SPEED

Speed is a measure of how quickly something is moving, or how fast it moves over a distance.

VELOCITY

Scientists think of velocity as not only an object's speed, but also the direction an object is going.

ACCELERATION

Acceleration measures the change in an object's velocity. Acceleration includes speeding up, slowing down and changing direction.

CENTER OF MASS

Many objects behave like their mass (how much matter they have) is focused at one point—this is called their center of mass. In a ball, it's right in the middle. However, for us humans, our center of mass is a little above our waist as we have more weight in the top half of our body. If you balance a book on a round pencil, the book's center of mass is right above the pencil.

A racing car has a low center of mass to stop it from tipping over as it quickly turns corners.

RAW OR HARD-BOILED?

How can you tell if an egg is raw or hard-boiled just by spinning it? It's all to do with its center of mass. A raw egg will wobble while it spins as the liquid moves inside the shell, changing its center of mass. A hard-boiled egg is solid so has a fixed center of mass and will spin smoothly.

MOMENTUM

Momentum is the combination of how fast something is moving with how much mass it has. Even though a tennis ball has less mass than a basketball, a tennis ball that's been hit hard has more momentum than a three-point shot because the tennis ball is going so much faster.

WALK THE TIGHTROPE

A tightrope walker has to understand balance and center of mass to complete this impressive act! To help them balance they often carry a long pole. With small movements, a tightrope walker can keep their, and the pole's, center of mass directly above the tightrope. This helps, but they can fall if they lose this balance.

EGG TATTOO

Chemical reactions are around us every day. They are how plants grow, soap cleans and food becomes energy for you to grow. In this experiment, we create a chemical reaction to write a message on an egg.

MATERIALS

- wax crayon
- hard-boiled egg in shell
- bowl
- measuring cup
- vinegar
- bowl of water
- spoon
- old toothbrush

TIMING

6 hours

1. Use a wax crayon to write your name or any short message on the shell of a hard-boiled egg.

2. Put the egg in a bowl. Use the beaker to pour in enough vinegar to cover the whole egg.

TIP
You can add food coloring to the vinegar for a rainbow-colored egg!

3. The vinegar creates a chemical reaction with the shell, causing bubbles to appear. Wait two hours, or until the bubbles stop. Empty out the old vinegar and refill the bowl with fresh vinegar, again covering the entire egg.

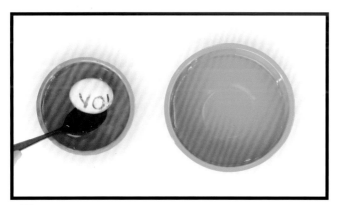

4. Wait four hours, or until the bubbles stop. Empty out the vinegar and remove the egg. Gently rinse the egg in a bowl of water.

5. Using a toothbrush, gently scrub the egg to remove the crayon from the shell. What do you see on the egg?

HOW IT WORKS

When two substances are combined and form a new substance, the process is called a CHEMICAL REACTION. Household vinegar is mainly ACETIC ACID and water. An eggshell is made of CALCIUM CARBONATE (KAL-see-um KAR-buh-nate). If acetic acid and calcium carbonate are combined, a chemical reaction takes place. When you placed your egg in vinegar, you started a chemical reaction between the calcium carbonate and the acetic acid. The eggshell starts to dissolve, and carbon dioxide gas is produced, creating bubbles. By writing on the eggshell with wax crayon first, you protected that small part of the eggshell from acetic acid. This means your message was saved while the rest of the eggshell began to dissolve.

DID YOU KNOW?

A pearl is mainly made of calcium carbonate.

GOOEY SLIME

VISCOSITY
(vi-SKOS-i-tee)

Have you ever watched honey ooze slowly out of a bottle and wondered why it is so slow? It's because of honey's viscosity. In this activity, we make some delightfully disgusting slime to explore viscosity.

MATERIALS

NOTE
This project can get messy, so you should work outside or put down some old newspaper before you begin.

- large mixing bowl
- measuring cup
- 125 ml (1/2 cup) warm water
- 125 ml (1/2 cup) clear or white washable school glue
- liquid coloring
- baking soda
- spoon or spatula
- 8 ml saline solution (contact lens solution, containing boric acid and sodium borate)

TIMING

20 minutes

1. In a large mixing bowl, add warm water, glue, several drops of liquid coloring and mix well.

2. Add a spoonful of baking soda and mix well.

3. Add saline solution and mix well.

4. Adjust the consistency of your slime by adding either more baking soda or water. What does the slime feel like?

HOW IT WORKS

How quickly or slowly a liquid flows is described as **VISCOSITY**. Honey and molasses are both very viscous, so they flow slowly. Water and milk are not very viscous, so they flow quickly. The viscosity of your slime was affected by the pressure you applied. If you handled your slime gently and let it ooze through your fingers, the molecules were able to move around freely. This made your slime feel gooey. But if you squeezed your slime tightly, the molecules became packed together. This made your slime feel solid.

IN REAL LIFE

Humans can't walk on water—but what about if you add cornstarch? If you mix water and cornstarch you make a substance called oobleck. Oobleck is a dilatant (dye-LAY-tent) material, which means the more you push on it, the stiffer it becomes. And thanks to the properties of a dilatant material (also known as a non-Newtonian fluid) if you fill a swimming pool with oobleck, you can walk across it. Just don't stop or you'll sink!

DID YOU KNOW?

Vegetable oil, water and air are all Newtonian fluids—Issac Newton himself investigated the way fluids like these work. Your slime, oobleck, ketchup and toothpaste are all examples of non-Newtonian fluids. Slime and oobleck are dilatant, but ketchup and toothpaste are thixotropic (thik-sugh-TRAW-pik). This means the more you push on them, the thinner they become.

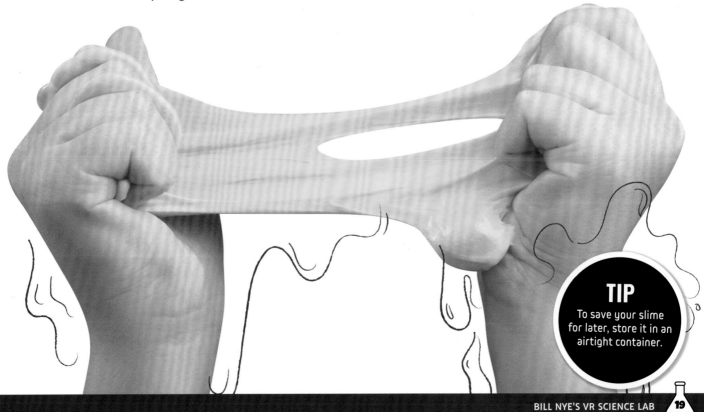

TIP
To save your slime for later, store it in an airtight container.

SOAPY TRICKS

SURFACE TENSION

Have you ever wondered how some insects can walk on water? It has to do with something called surface tension. In this project, let's investigate how soap affects the surface tension of water.

MATERIALS

- shallow dish
- water
- black pepper
- liquid dish soap
- string

TIMING

15 minutes

1. Fill a shallow dish partway with water. Sprinkle black pepper on the water's surface. Watch how the pepper spreads.

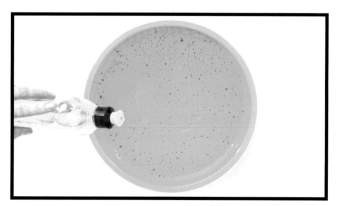

2. Add a drop of liquid dish soap to one side of the dish. What happens to the pepper now?

LET'S TRY IT A DIFFERENT WAY!

3. Rinse out the dish and start with a new bowl of water. Tie a piece of string and float it on the surface of the water. Add a drop of liquid dish soap inside the string. What happens to the loop of string?

HOW IT WORKS

Similar molecules tend to be attracted to each other rather than different types of molecules. Water molecules stick together especially tightly at the water's surface, because they're more attracted to the other water molecules than to the molecules in the air. At the water's surface, they form a layer that acts like an elastic sheet. This is **SURFACE TENSION**. When you added soap to the water and pepper, you lowered the water's surface tension. The soap made the top layer of water molecules spread out quickly, carrying the pepper with them. In the second version of the experiment, the surface tension of the water around the string is higher than the soapy water inside so the string is pulled into a circular shape.

IN REAL LIFE

Some bugs can walk on water because they don't weigh enough to break the surface tension of water. Surface tension also explains why a wet tent stays dry inside until it's touched. Touching the tent on the inside breaks the surface tension of the water droplets on the outside, which causes water to leak in.

DID YOU KNOW?

When you wash your hands with soap and water, one end of a soap molecule sticks to water while the other end sticks to oily things, like the fatty outer layers of viruses and bacteria. When you rinse your hands, they are then washed away. Washing your hands thoroughly with soap and water is the best way to keep from getting sick.

LAVA LAMP

DENSITY

Why does salad dressing always have a layer of oil sitting at the top of the bottle? It's all because of density! In this activity, we create our own lava lamp to learn about different densities.

MATERIALS

- measuring cup
- clear bottle
- water
- funnel
- vegetable oil
- liquid coloring
- effervescent antacid tablet

TIMING

20 minutes

1. Use the beaker to fill the bottle about 1/4 full with water.

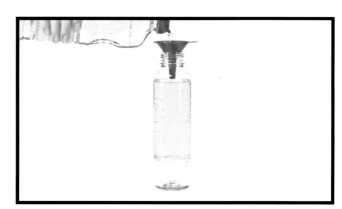

2. Using the funnel, add the oil until the bottle is nearly full.

BE PATIENT!

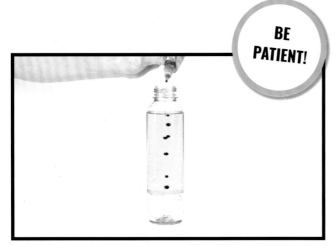

3. Add 10-12 drops of liquid coloring. Watch as the food coloring slowly falls through the oil and mixes with the water.

4. Break an effervescent antacid tablet into six small pieces, and drop them into the bottle one by one. What happens?

TIP
When the bubbling stops, add another piece of the antacid tablet. Enjoy the show again!

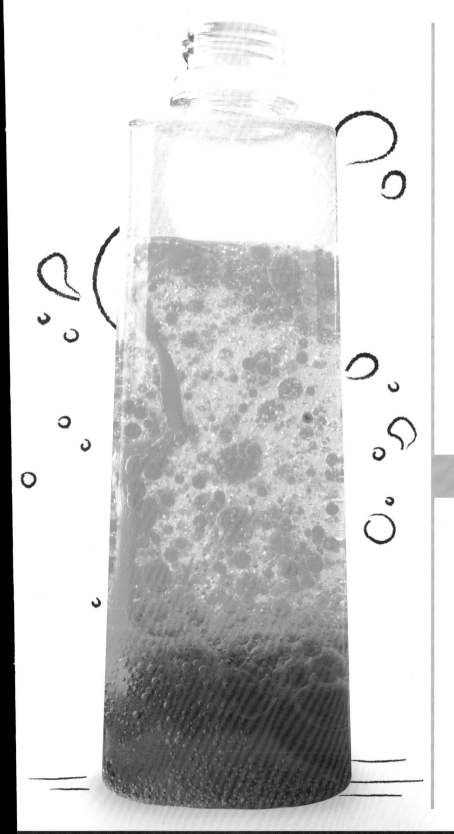

IN REAL LIFE

Sometimes, a tanker ship filled with oil has an accident and spills oil into the ocean. Because oil is less dense than water, the oil floats on the ocean's surface. This makes it a bit easier for the clean-up crew to do their job, but cleaning up after an oil spill is still very difficult.

HOW IT WORKS

Water molecules are small, so they can pack together tightly. Oil molecules are larger, so they can't pack together as closely. This means that water is DENSER than oil and will separate into a distinct layer below the oil. If you shake the bottle, the oil and water still won't mix. When you dropped a tablet into the bottle, it reacted with the water producing bubbles of carbon dioxide gas. These bubbles are less dense than oil so they rose to the top, taking colored water with them. When the bubbles reached the top, they escaped into the air and left the colored water behind. As water is more dense than oil, the water fell back down to the bottom.

Let's talk about...
DENSITY

Density is how much space an object or substance takes up (its volume) in relation to the amount of matter in that object or substance (its mass).

DENSITY PARFAIT

Liquids can all be measured by their density. For example, we know that oil is less dense than water so it will float on top. If liquids of different densities are poured slowly into a beaker they will create distinct layers. This reveals how dense each liquid is.

FLOATING OBJECTS

As with liquids, objects also have density. If items are dropped into the parfait, each will sink to a liquid level of the same density.

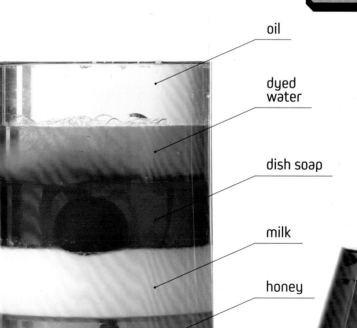

oil

dyed water

dish soap

milk

honey

The Dead Sea is almost 10 times saltier than most oceans.

SALT vs. FRESH WATER

If salt is dissolved in fresh water, the density of that water increases. This is because the mass, or amount of "stuff," in the water increases while the volume, or "size," stays almost the same. The more salt that is added to water, the more dense it becomes. An egg will sink in water but if you add salt, the water increases in density until eventually the egg is less dense and will float to the top.

DEAD SEA

The Dead Sea is a salt lake and the lowest body of water on Earth at around 1,410 feet (430 m) below sea level. The water in the Dead Sea is very high in salt, it is almost 10 times saltier than most oceans. This means the water is very dense and if you visit the Dead Sea, you will float like a ping pong ball in a bathtub! The water is so salty that no fish, algae or plants can survive, giving the lake its name.

DISPLACEMENT

When in water, a boat will displace or push away some of the water. The weight of the water displaced exactly equals the weight of the boat. The denser the water, the less of it a boat has to displace to float. Huge cruise ships carry over 6,000 passengers as well as crew, food, fuel, water, cargo and the ship's machinery. These giants of the sea have to be carefully designed to ensure that they will float in waters of different densities.

HEAT RISING

Now you have learned about density, can you predict what will happen in this experiment?

MATERIALS

- Two glass cups
- cold water
- hot water
- red and blue liquid coloring
- straw

TIMING

10 minutes

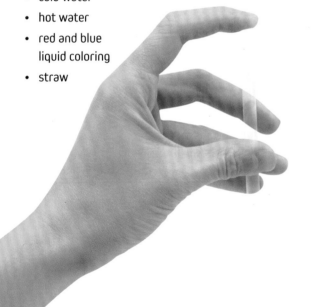

TIP
Add ice to the cold water!

ASK AN ADULT!

1. Fill a glass with cold water. Ask an adult to fill a second glass with hot water.

2. Add a few drops of blue liquid coloring to the cold water and red liquid coloring to the hot water. ■ Gently mix the color in each glass.

DID YOU KNOW?

Blow up a balloon and it will fall to the ground, but fill it with helium and it will float. This is because helium is less dense than the air around it. Helium is mined from wells found deep under the Earth's surface.

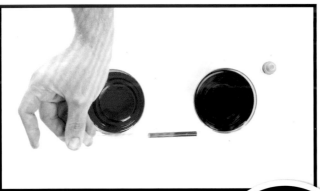

3. Carefully dip about a quarter of the straw into the hot water. Hold your finger over the top of the straw and take it out of the water.

4. Dip the straw about halfway into the cold water. Lift off your finger then quickly put it back over the top. With your finger covering the top of the straw, pull it out of the water. What do you see?

NOTE
Keep your finger over the top of the straw while it is out of the water!

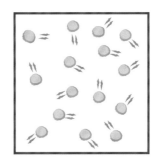 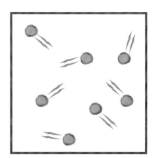

The same volume of cold water contains more molecules, making it denser than warm water.

When you heat up water, the water molecules start to move faster. The fast-moving molecules bounce off each other and move further apart. This means in the same volume of warm and cold water, the warm water has fewer molecules, so it is less dense. The cold water squeezes the warm water up.

Similar to water, as air molecules warm up they start to vibrate and bump into each other, moving further apart. This means the air expands, becoming less dense and is squeezed above the cold air. This is why the second floor of a house is often warmer than downstairs.

IN REAL LIFE

Hot air balloons use, you guessed it, hot air. Air inside the balloon (called the envelope) is heated with a burner and this warm air is surrounded by colder air outside. The cold air squeezes the warm air up, which lifts the balloon higher. As the air cools, the balloon will slowly lower. The envelope is kept inflated while in flight as the heated air has more pressure than the air outside the balloon envelope.

BLUBBER GLOVE

Insulation is vital to keep things warm—from your body to your house. In this project, learn about insulation and compare the insulating properties of water and fat.

MATERIALS

- two medium resealable plastic bags
- duct tape
- funnel
- vegetable oil
- large bowl of icy water

TIMING

15 minutes

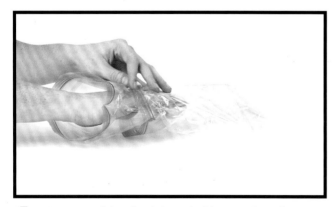

1. Turn one of the plastic bags inside out. Place the inside-out bag inside the second plastic bag.

2. Seal the zippers of the two plastic bags together, leaving one section unsealed. Tape the tops of the two plastic bags together. Do not tape over the unsealed gap.

TIP
You might need a second person to help hold the funnel or pour the oil.

3. Place the funnel in the unsealed gap between the bags. Carefully pour vegetable oil into the funnel, stopping when the outer plastic bag is about 2/3 full.

4. Finish zipping the two plastic bags together. Tape over the gap to seal the bags.

5. Place one hand in icy water. How long does it take before your hand gets uncomfortable? Wait a few minutes, until your hand feels normal again. Put your hand inside the plastic bag so it is surrounded by oil, then place it in the icy water. Now how long does it take before your hand feels uncomfortable?

HOW IT WORKS

A material that doesn't allow heat to escape easily is called an INSULATOR (IN-su-lay-ter). Fat is a good insulator and water is a poor insulator. When you plunged your hand in icy water, the heat from your hand quickly escaped into the water. But when you wrapped your hand in the oil-filled plastic bags, you protected your hand with fat before plunging it into the icy water. The fat in the oil acted as an insulator so the heat escaped more slowly from your hand.

IN REAL LIFE

Marine mammals such as whales, seals and walruses have a thick layer of fat under their skin, called blubber. Blubber has a lot of fat stored in it, but fibers also help it hold its shape. This blubber helps marine mammals survive in the ice-cold Arctic and Antarctic waters.

FUN FACT

People who live in Arctic regions sometimes eat muktuk, which is a dish made from frozen whale skin and raw blubber.

SUPER SPEAKERS

Do you know why music played from a smartphone sometimes sounds funny? It is because of the way sound waves travel. In this project, you can build your own set of speakers, and learn how this affects the sound waves.

MATERIALS

- cardboard tube
- felt pen
- smartphone
- scissors
- two paper cups
- duct tape
- two sheets of paper towel

TIMING

60 minutes

FUN FACT

Which is louder, a rocket ship blasting off or 10 million rock bands performing at the same time? The rocket ship is louder!

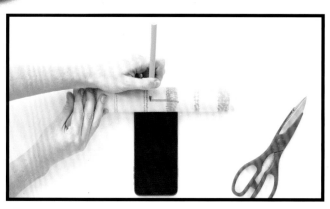

1. Halfway along the cardboard tube, use the felt pen to trace around the end of your smartphone. Make a flap by cutting along the two short sides and one long side of the shape you just drew. Fold up the flap.

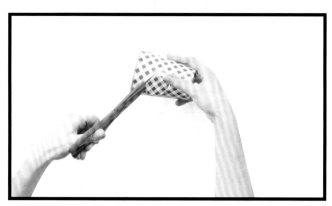

2. Near the lip of one of the paper cups, use the felt pen to trace around the end of the cardboard tube. Repeat with the other cup. Cut out the two circles.

3. Place a few pieces of tape inside one end of the tube. Push that end of the tube into the hole in one of the paper cups. Tape the tube and cup together. Repeat on the other end of the tube using the other cup.

4. Loosely crumple two sheets of paper towel. Place in each end of the cardboard tube, inside the cups.

5. Place your smartphone into the slot so that its speaker is inside the cardboard tube. Play a song.
■ How does it sound?

HOW IT WORKS

When objects vibrate, they create sound waves. These SOUND WAVES can travel through air, water and even solid objects. The sound waves reach our ears and make our eardrums vibrate, which our brains recognize as sound. When music plays from a smartphone it spreads out quickly from the small speaker inside, especially the low notes. When you placed your smartphone in the cardboard speakers, the sound waves bounced off the insides of the tube and cups and were funneled in one direction, toward you. The paper towel absorbed some of the high-pitched sounds but let the low-pitched sounds through. This makes the music sound more like the way it sounded when it was recorded.

IN REAL LIFE

Dogs can hear high-pitched sounds that humans can't hear. This is why a dog responds to the high-pitched sound of a dog whistle, but we can't hear it.

DANCING PAPER

Sometimes static electricity can be shocking! In this experiment, we create our own static electricity by rubbing a balloon and making paper dance.

MATERIALS

- piece of paper
- scissors or hole punch
- balloon

TIMING

20 minutes

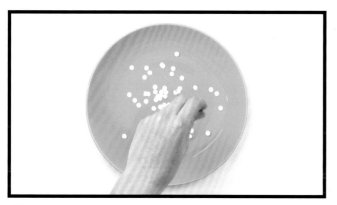

1. Using scissors or a hole punch, cut out about 20 small pieces of paper. Spread out the pieces on a table or a flat surface.

2. Blow up the balloon and tie a knot in it.

3. Rub the balloon on a wool blanket (or your hair), back and forth for about 10 seconds.

4. Hold the balloon slightly above the small pieces of paper. What happens?

HOW IT WORKS

Every physical object is made up of tiny atoms which contain protons, neutrons and electrons. Usually atoms have the same number of protons and electrons but when you rub the balloon on your hair or a blanket, some electrons end up on the surface of the balloon and stay there, so we call them static. These unbalanced charges cause **STATIC ELECTRICITY** to build up on the balloon's surface. The static electricity created was strong enough to attract the paper to the balloon.

FUN FACT

Lightning can be a very powerful and dangerous type of static electricity. The temperature in a lightning bolt can reach 50,000°F (30,000°C)!

STICKY ICE

Have you ever wondered why icy roads are covered with salt in winter? Salt changes the melting point of ice so in this project, we experiment with adding salt to an ice cube.

MATERIALS

- ice cubes
- plate
- salt
- string
- water

TIMING

15 minutes

1. Place an ice cube on a plate, and sprinkle some salt on top of the ice.

2. Place a second ice cube on top of the first one, and press down firmly for one minute.

3. Try to lift the top ice cube. What happens?

LET'S TRY IT A DIFFERENT WAY!

4. Soak a piece of string in water. Place a new ice cube on a plate, then lay the wet string on top. Sprinkle salt over the top of the ice cube, covering the string.

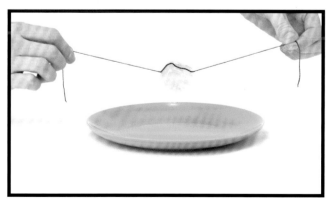

5. Wait one minute, then pick up the string by both ends and lift. What happens?

DID YOU KNOW?

Melting point and freezing point are the same thing! When the temperature climbs above 32°F (0°C), ice melts and becomes water. When the temperature drops below 32°F (0°C), water freezes and becomes ice.

HOW IT WORKS

The temperature at which water changes from solid ice to liquid water is called the MELTING POINT. For water it is 32°F (0°C) but salt lowers this temperature. When you sprinkled salt on the wet string and ice cube, you changed the melting point and it began to melt a little. The melted water was still very cold, so it refreezes to stick to the second ice cube or around the string, allowing you to pick up the first ice cube.

Let's talk about...
TEMPERATURE

Have you ever jumped into a pool on a hot day and felt cold? This is thanks to the way our body feels temperature.

HOT OR COLD?

Temperature PERCEPTION (per-SEP-shun) is the way our bodies sense heat or cold. Our brain processes temperature by using temperature RECEPTORS (rih-SEP-terz) in our skin. These receptors are activated when we jump in a pool but our perception is affected by our environment. On a hot day a pool will feel cold, but on a cold day it will feel relatively warmer. If we stay in the water, our receptors stop working as hard and we don't sense the temperature as much. This is called DESENSITIZATION (dee-sen-si-tuh-ZAY-shun).

MEASURING TEMPERATURE

The two most common scales for measuring temperature are Celsius or centigrade (°C) and Fahrenheit (°F). These are commonly used for weather reporting. The range 0°C to 100°C corresponds to the freezing and boiling points of water at sea level, equivalent to 32°F and 212°F. The only point these two scales are equal is at -40 degrees.

F°	C°
140	60
122	50
104	40
86	30
68	20
50	10
32	0
14	-10
-4	-20
-22	-30
-40	-40
-58	-50
-76	-60

FUN FACT
134°F (56.7°C)
Highest recorded temperature on Earth
-128.6°F (-89.2°C)
Lowest recorded temperature on Earth

STRETCHING TOWER

On hot, summer days, the Eiffel Tower in France can grow up to 6 inches (15 cm) taller! When steel is put under high temperatures, it undergoes thermal expansion. So when temperatures reach as high as 100°F (40°C) the heat causes the steel at the Eiffel Tower's base to expand and the tower "grows." When temperatures cool, the steel contracts again and the tower shrinks.

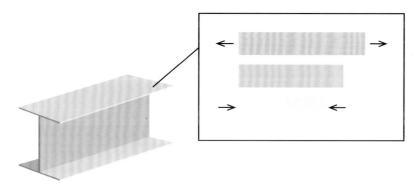

Steel expands under extreme heat and will contract as temperatures cool.

FROZEN FROGS

Wood frogs live in northern areas of North America, including Arctic Canada and Alaska. In winter, something quite strange happens— the frogs freeze! As winter approaches they produce glucose (sugar) which acts as a sort of anti-freeze. As temperatures drop, their heart stops beating but the glucose keeps them alive. Once the temperature rises, their heart starts to beat again and they are ready for spring!

BODY TEMPERATURE

The average human body temperature is around 98°F (37°C) and our bodies are very good at regulating temperature. If we get too hot, blood vessels in our skin widen to take excess heat to the surface. We will also sweat which helps to cool our body as it evaporates. If we get too cold, the blood vessels narrow to reduce blood flow to the skin's surface where it would cool. We will also often shiver when we are cold. This trembling of the muscles actually helps to produce heat and warm us up.

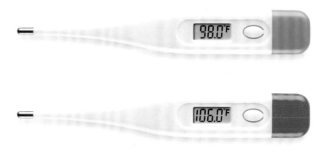

A high temperature, or fever, is one way our bodies deal with an infection.

LEAK-PROOF BAG

It might sound like a magic trick, but you can make holes in a water-filled plastic bag without spilling any water. In this experiment, we learn about polymers to find out how.

MATERIALS

- pencil sharpener
- 4-6 pencils
- resealable plastic bag
- water

TIMING

5 minutes

NOTE
Use smooth round pencils. Other pencils don't work as well.

TIP
You might want to try this experiment outside or over the kitchen sink, just in case of spills!

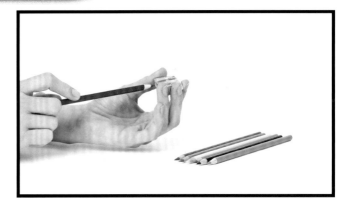

1. Use the pencil sharpener to sharpen each pencil to a point.

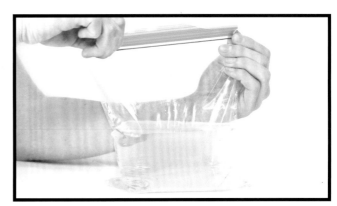

2. Fill the resealable plastic bag half full of water, and seal the bag.

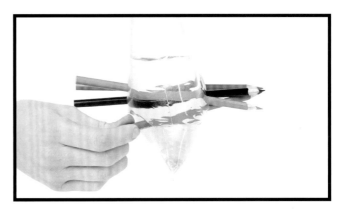

3. Push each pencil through one side of the bag and halfway out the other side. What happens?

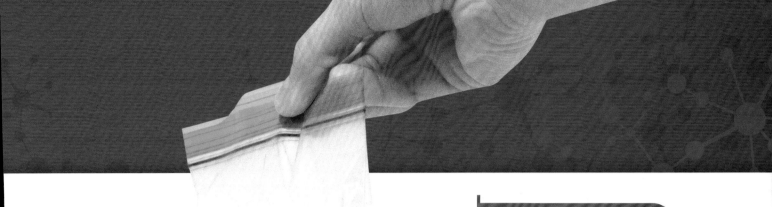

HOW IT WORKS

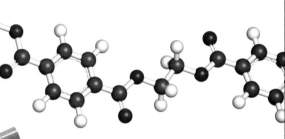

A different polymer, PET (polyethylene terephthalate), is commonly used to make plastic bottles.

Long, flexible chains of molecules are called **POLYMERS**. Most plastic bags are made from a polymer called **POLYETHYLENE** (pah-lee-EH-thuh-lean). Each time you poked pencils into the bag, you pushed apart the polyethylene molecules. These molecules are so flexible that they formed temporary seals around each pencil, which stopped the water from getting out. But make sure to place the bag in the sink before removing any pencils! You permanently pushed apart the molecules and the water will gush out.

IN REAL LIFE

Synthetic polymers make up a huge number of different plastics. Water bottles, toys, plastic cutlery and food packaging are just some examples of plastic we use every day. Plastic has many useful qualities but we now know it poses a real risk to our environment. Reducing our use and recycling are simple steps we can all take to help the environment.

DID YOU KNOW?

A polymer is a chemical substance that is made up of small molecules that are arranged to form a larger molecule. You can have natural and artificial polymers.

ACID vs BASE

Why do lemons and vinegar taste sour?
What does baking powder do in a cake mix?
Let's learn about acids and bases.

VEGETABLE INDICATOR

Did you know that you can determine whether
something is an acid or a base using hot
water and red cabbage? The color of the
liquid will indicate the level of acid or base
in everyday items. This is thanks to a
water-soluble pigment, ANTHOCYANIN
(an-thuh-SIGH-ah-nin), that changes
color when mixed with
an acid or base. Acid
will turn the solution red
while base causes
blue-green colors.

DID YOU KNOW?
The word anthocyanin comes from the Greek and German for "blue flower."

ACIDIC   NEUTRAL   BASIC

BASE OR ALKALI?

A base is a substance that reacts with acids and neutralizes them.
Many bases are insoluble—they will not dissolve in water. If a base
does dissolve in water, it is also called an alkali. All alkalis are bases,
but only soluble bases are alkalis.

ACID POWER

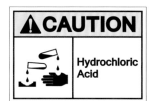

Hydrochloric acid is a very strong acid, used for industrial and home cleaning products. It is so strong that it can burn through stainless steel. Products that contain hydrochloric acid must be used with great care. This acid also makes up part of gastric acid—the acid in our stomach that breaks down the food we eat. To protect us from damage, our stomach produces a mucus.

Hydrochloric acid is a water-based solution of the elements hydrogen (H) and chlorine (Cl).

ACID RAIN

Acid rain damage.

As rain falls, it reacts with carbon dioxide in the air and some rainwater becomes weak carbonic acid, which makes rain have a pH around 5. However, burning fossil fuels such as coal, oil and natural gas releases sulfur oxide, nitrogen dioxide and carbon dioxide into the atmosphere, all of which lower the pH of rain. Acid rain can cause damage to plants and wildlife, erode certain buildings and cause iron to rust.

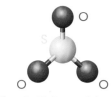

Sulfur trioxide is one of the main components of acid rain. It is made up of the elements sulfur (S) and oxygen (O).

SWEET SCIENCE

You may not know, but when you bake a cake you are actually performing a science experiment! Baking powder, which is added to a cake batter, contains an acid and a base. When water is added to the mix and then it is heated, they react producing small carbon dioxide bubbles that make the cake rise. Science never tasted so good!

DID YOU KNOW?

Different plants prefer different levels of acid or base in their soil. When farmers grow crops, they carefully monitor pH levels and can add fertilizers to reduce the pH, or add bases to raise the soil pH.

COPPER COINS

When a copper penny gets old, it tends to look dull and green. This is thanks to a process called oxidation. In this experiment, see oxidation in action with the help of some vinegar.

MATERIALS

- paper towels
- bowl
- pennies
- white vinegar
- beaker
- tweezers

TIMING

2 days

1. Fold a couple of pieces of paper towel and place in a bowl. Put the pennies on top of the paper towel.

2. Pour the white vinegar over the pennies, making sure the paper towel is well soaked.

3. Wait at least 24 hours before checking your pennies. What do you notice?

TIP
If your paper towel gets too dry, add more vinegar.

HOW IT WORKS

When copper is exposed to water and oxygen for a long time, it changes color from brown to green in a process called OXIDATION. The green film that forms on copper is called COPPER OXIDE. Adding vinegar to the copper pennies starts a chemical reaction that speeds up the process of oxidation. The blue-green substance you created is called MALACHITE (MAL-uh-kite).

Minneapolis City Hall, Minnesota

LOOK AROUND

Just like the Statue of Liberty, many buildings around the world have green roofs thanks to the oxidation of copper. Berlin Cathedral Church, the Millennium Centre in Wales and Minneapolis City Hall are all examples of buildings that use copper in their design.

CHASING RAINBOWS

REFRACTION
(ruh-FRAK-shun)

Seeing a rainbow in the sky when the Sun comes out on a rainy day is a beautiful sight. Did you know we see rainbows because of reflection and refraction? In this activity, we'll make our own rainbow and learn about light refracting.

MATERIALS

- shallow dish
- water
- mirror
- white paper
- a sunny day!

TIMING

10 minutes

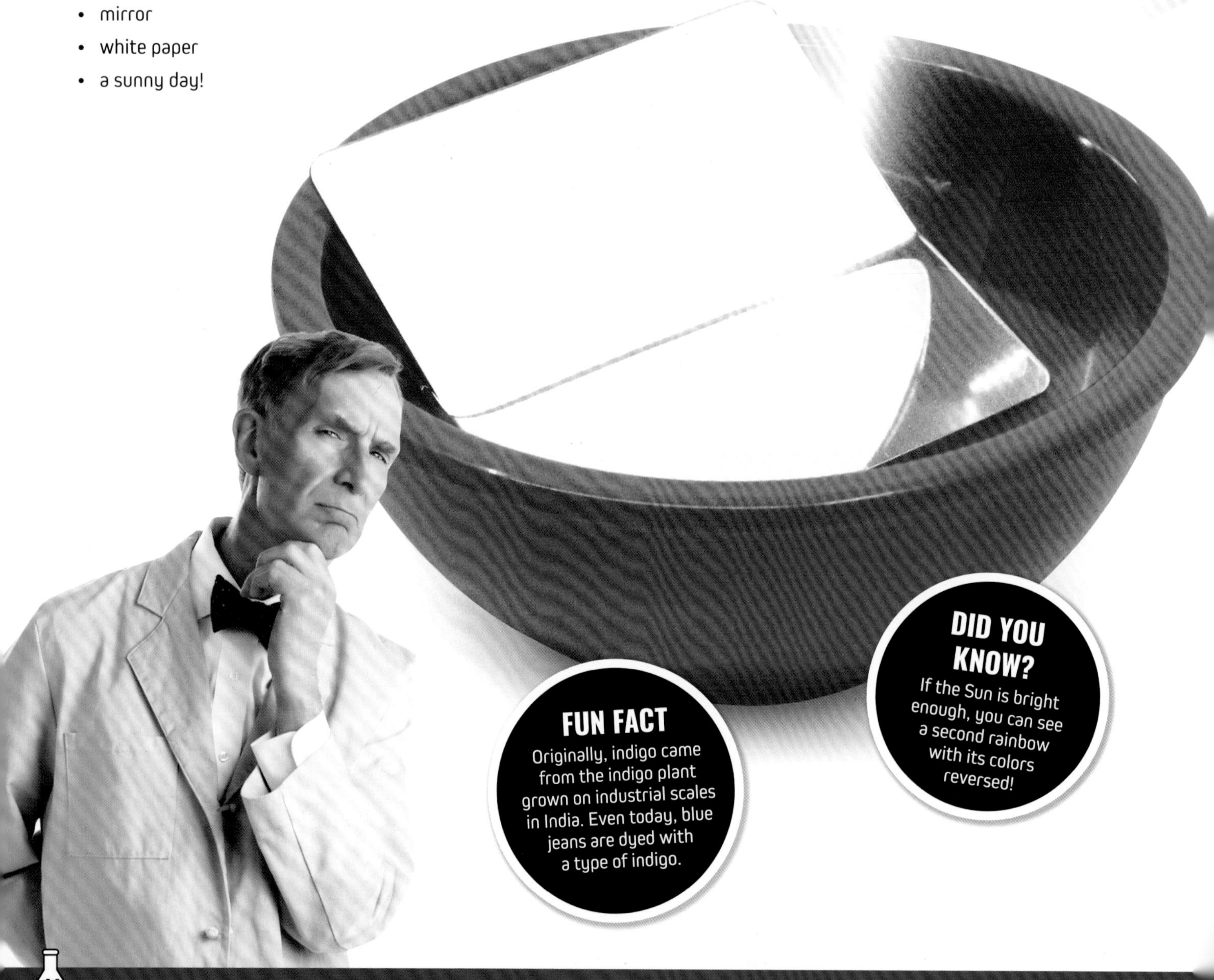

FUN FACT
Originally, indigo came from the indigo plant grown on industrial scales in India. Even today, blue jeans are dyed with a type of indigo.

DID YOU KNOW?
If the Sun is bright enough, you can see a second rainbow with its colors reversed!

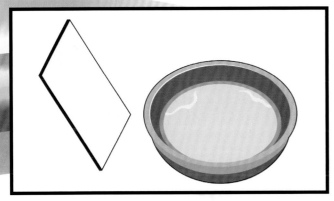

1. Fill a shallow dish with water. Place the mirror inside the dish.

2. Position the dish so that the Sun shines onto the mirror.

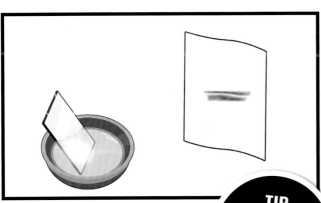

3. Hold up a sheet of white paper and face it toward the mirror. ▪ What happens?

TIP
If you can't see a rainbow, move the mirror around a bit.

HOW IT WORKS

Light from the Sun looks white, but it is actually made up of all the colors of the rainbow: red, orange, yellow, green, blue, indigo and violet. Light rays usually travel in a straight line, but they bend when they pass from one substance (such as air) to another substance (such as water). This bending is called REFRACTION. When light refracts and reflects through water, the light disperses and a rainbow forms. In your experiment, sunlight refracted when it hit water, then it reflected off the mirror and dispersed into the seven colors of the rainbow on the paper.

DID YOU KNOW?

When viewed from an airplane high in the sky, we can see a rainbow as a full circle instead of a semicircle from the ground.

FUN FACT

ROY G BIV is an easy way to remember the colors of the rainbow—red, orange, yellow, green, blue, indigo, violet.

TRAPPING GAS

Have you ever noticed that soda sometimes makes you burp? It is because of carbon dioxide, which is what makes soda fizzy. In this project, we use the power of carbon dioxide to inflate a balloon.

MATERIALS

- bottle of soda
- balloon
- rubber band

TIMING

10 minutes

1 Remove the cap from the bottle of soda. Quickly stretch the opening of the balloon over the mouth of the bottle.

2 Wrap the rubber band around the end of the balloon a few times and make sure it fits tightly on the bottle.

3 Pick up the bottle and gently shake it then place it back down. You can also tap the bottom of the bottle on a table. What happens to the balloon?

SOUND LIKE A SCIENTIST

The chemical formula for carbon dioxide is CO_2. This means that it contains one atom of carbon and two atoms of oxygen.

HOW IT WORKS

Two of the most important gases are oxygen and carbon dioxide. They both have no color, no smell and no taste. We breathe in OXYGEN and breathe out CARBON DIOXIDE. Trees and plants do the opposite: they take in carbon dioxide and release clean oxygen back into the air. To make soda, carbon dioxide is forced into flavored water at a very high pressure. When you opened your bottle of soda, you released some of that pressure and the carbon dioxide bubbles rose to the top of the liquid. When you shook the soda, you gave the carbon dioxide more energy to escape the liquid. This created even more bubbles, which quickly escaped the bottle and got trapped in the balloon, making it inflate.

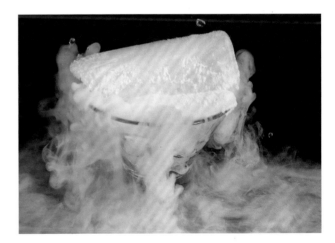

DID YOU KNOW?

Frozen carbon dioxide is called dry ice. It is much colder than regular ice made from water, so it works well to keep items cold for long periods of time (for example, frozen food shipped across the country). When dry ice warms up, it doesn't turn into a big watery mess, like regular ice. Instead, dry ice turns back into a gas.

AIR PRESSURE

Air pressure is the force on a surface caused by the air molecules above.

RISING WATER

A classic experiment: when a candle is burning, there's warm air, carbon dioxide and water vapor above it. As you lower a glass over the candle, the glass fills with this warm mixture of gases and the candle keeps burning. As the candle runs out of oxygen, it starts to dim and the gases in the glass start to cool and contract. When the candle finally goes out, the gases cool quickly, and atmospheric pressure forces some of the surrounding water up under the rim of the glass.

DID YOU KNOW?

Egyptian diver Ahmed Gabr holds the world record for deepest scuba dive. He reached an amazing 1,090 feet 4.5 in. (332.35 m) in the Red Sea, off the coast of Egypt.

UP IN THE AIR

The higher above the Earth's surface you travel, the lower the air pressure as there is less air above pressing down. When you take off in an airplane, it is common for your ears to pop as air pressure changes. The air pressure in an airplane's cabin is somewhat lower than on the ground. If we made planes strong enough to hold the same air pressure as on the ground, planes would be too heavy to fly very well.

A barometer reads air pressure and can predict if a storm is coming.

PREDICTING STORMS

Air pressure can be measured using a tool called a BAROMETER (buh-RAW-muh-ter). Air pressure moves in predictable ways from high to low pressure and barometers show these changes. Since storms form in low air pressure, they can be useful in predicting when a storm is approaching.

Oxygen tanks help divers breathe underwater.

DEEP DIVE

Pressure under water increases with depth. Qualified scuba divers can normally reach a maximum depth of -130 feet (-40 m). Even at this depth, the pressure is five times that at sea level. The pressure causes the lungs to contract making breathing extremely difficult. To combat this, divers use tanks filled with compressed, oxygen-rich air to help them breathe.

MARIANA TRENCH

The deepest known point in Earth's ocean, the Mariana Trench is 35,756 feet (10,898 m) deep. The pressure is more than a thousand times that at sea level.

RADICAL CRYSTALS

STALACTITES AND STALAGMITES
(stuh-LAK-tites)
(stuh-LAG-mites)

Stalactites and stalagmites are amazing mineral formations found in caves. A stalactite grows down from the ceiling of a cave and a stalagmite grows up from the floor. In this activity, you can make your own crystal stalactites.

MATERIALS

- three pieces of string, each about 10 inches (25 cm) long
- two washers
- two glasses
- hot tap water
- baking soda
- measuring spoon
- food coloring
- plate

TIMING

Three days

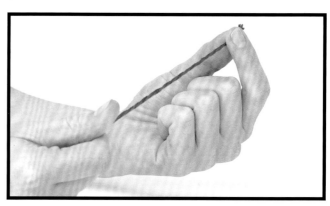

1. Twist together the three pieces of string to form one thick string.

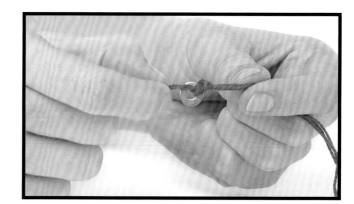

2. Tie a washer onto each end of the thick string.

TIP
If you wait long enough you will see stalagmites forming on the plate!

Reed Flute Cave, China

3. Carefully fill the two glasses with hot tap water. Add four spoonfuls of baking soda into each glass. Quickly stir the solution to dissolve as much baking soda as possible.

4. Add several drops of food coloring to the solution, and stir.

5. Put a plate between the two glasses. Drop each end of the string into the glasses so that the washers are underwater. Leave it for several days, checking back daily. What forms in the middle of the string?

IN REAL LIFE

Caves full of stalactites are popular tourist attractions around the world. Reed Flute Cave in China is more than 180 million years old, and its stalactites have attracted visitors for over 1,200 years.

SOUND LIKE A SCIENTIST

To keep from mixing up the two words, remember that stalactites hold **tight** to the ceiling; stalagmites **might** reach them.

HOW IT WORKS

A long, thin column of minerals that hangs from the ceiling of a cave is called a stalactite. It can take many centuries for a stalactite to form, as water slowly drips through the cave's ceiling and leaves behind large deposits of minerals. In your experiment, the solution of water and baking soda travels along the string to meet in the middle. This formed tiny baking soda crystal stalactites.